The Snow Queen

Original story by Hans Christian Andersen
Retold by Chris Baker
Series Advisor Professor Kimberley Reynolds
Illustrated by Daniela Jaglenka Terrazzini

OXFORD
UNIVERSITY PRESS

Letter from the Author

I live in Oxfordshire with my family and a rabbit. When I'm not writing, I work with computers, and spend my free time doing martial arts.

Hans Christian Andersen published *The Snow Queen* in 1845, but it has the feeling of a traditional quest story. Quest stories have always been popular. They allow for lots of adventure, often of a dreamlike or fantastical kind. I think the best ones also put the hero into a situation we probably all recognize from real life: trying to do something we're not sure we can do, and needing to overcome our own weaknesses to succeed. I hope you enjoy adventuring with Gerda as she finds her strengths, meets friends (and people who only seemed to be friends), and finally gets to the point where ... well, read on and find out!

Chris Baker

A Boy and a Girl, a Mirror and its Pieces

The crow saw them, in fact, just before their part in the story began. Passing by the old town, it saw a boy and a girl talking together on a rose-covered balcony.

I should find out more about those two ... the crow thought to itself, and decided to come past again some time. It already had urgent business that afternoon, though, and so it did not see Gerda and Kai again until much later.

On the balcony, Gerda did not see the crow. She was lying on her back, arms behind her head with one leg stretched up. She turned her foot this way and that. She was enjoying the sunshine filtering through the leaves of the climbing roses, as they cascaded over the iron railings of the balcony. The sunshine was pleasantly warm, but the sun itself was just a bright sparkle through the leaves; she could cover it with her toes, and see the rose bush and its flowers. Then she could move her foot, and lose the roses in the sparkle of the sun. Her shoes were red and new – a birthday present this morning – and she could look from shiny leather to velvety, scented roses.

Her best friend and next-door neighbour Kai was propped up on an elbow nearby, getting just a little bored. He was happy, though – he'd made Gerda a chess set for her birthday, and she had loved it. *It was,* Kai thought in all honesty, *a good piece of work.* He had secretly collected offcuts from the carpenter and had whittled and carved and sanded for months. The white pieces were things from tales of the frozen north – jagged ice spires for the pawns, polar bears and wolves, an ice giant for the king, and, of course, the Snow Queen for the queen. Then he had collected some darker wood for the opposing side. These were from tales of the forests – roses for pawns, foxes and a fairy-tale prince and princess. Kai and Gerda had played several games with the set today. Kai had mostly won, of course, and luckily he'd managed not to lose his temper in the last game, when Gerda had taken his Snow Queen piece and queened one of her own rose pawns to win. Now Gerda was lost in – well, something. It seemed to be making her happy.

Kai fidgeted. 'We haven't read anything from that storybook I borrowed!' he said. 'We were so busy playing chess that I completely forgot about it. Let's read it now, or we won't have time before I have to take it back.'

Kai reached for the book. It was propped up by the iron gate between Gerda's balcony and Kai's. That gate had been left open for years. When they were younger, Kai and Gerda had squeaked it open and clanged it shut so often that their parents had agreed it would be better – certainly more peaceful – for there to be one big balcony shared by the two households. Now the gate was mostly overgrown by the exuberant climbing roses.

'You borrowed this book from someone at the carnival?' asked Gerda.

'Yes,' Kai said. 'I was nearly finished with the chessmen, but I couldn't get the Snow Queen right. She kept on coming out looking like you, I'm afraid! I heard the carnival had a storyteller this year, so yesterday I went to ask her what she thought the Snow Queen looked like. She thought it was really interesting that I wanted to know about the Snow Queen. She found a book that had a picture, and she said she would read it to me. But I said that I had to get back right away because I needed to finish your Snow Queen chess piece. So she said I could borrow the book – provided that I brought it back today. That's no problem, of course, since we said we'd go to the carnival this evening anyway. The storyteller said she knows lots of stories about the Snow Queen, and can tell me as much as I want to know!' Kai was thumbing through the pages of the storybook. 'Look,' he said, 'here's the Snow Queen. Isn't it an amazing picture?'

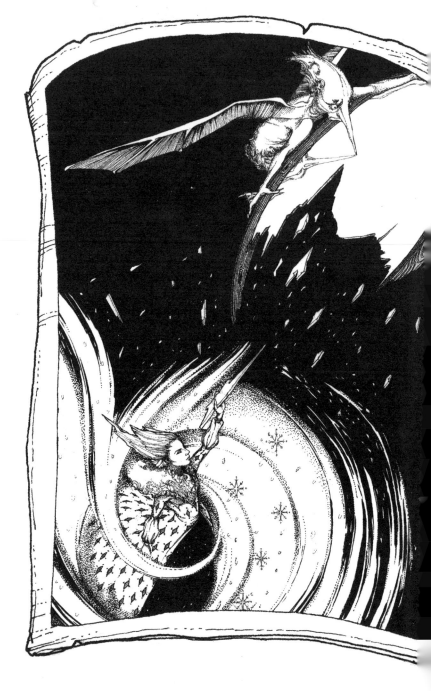

It was an amazing picture, but Gerda found it somehow unsettling. The Snow Queen was shown in the bottom left corner, standing in a snowy scene and holding up something shiny and spiky. Most of the picture, though, was of a flying hobgoblin. The hobgoblin was holding a mirror frame, but the mirror itself seemed to have just exploded into countless tiny pieces. These showered down across the scene, and where they reached the Snow Queen's part of the picture, the artist had cleverly made them change into snowflakes. So skilfully had it been done that Gerda couldn't see the point at which the pieces of mirror became ice and snow, even though she looked backwards and forwards until she began to feel mildly sick.

'I still don't think I got the Snow Queen quite right,' said Kai a bit sadly. 'She still looks a bit like you.'

Gerda gathered some of the chessmen. She could see Kai's point. But she was glad that Kai's Snow Queen didn't look exactly like the cruel and heartless woman in the book. She looked at the other chessmen – partly so that she didn't have to look at the illustration.

The king on the forest creatures' side did look a bit like Kai, come to think of it. Gerda knew it was ridiculous, but she suddenly felt cross that the Snow Queen piece looked more like her than the other queen did. She couldn't stop herself wondering whether the other queen looked more like anyone else they knew – an older girl, perhaps?

'You see, it can't be right if the Snow Queen looks like you, Gerda,' Kai was continuing, 'because the Snow Queen is a cruel monster, and you're the kindest person I know. But perhaps the storyteller will lend me the book for longer, and I can try making another Snow Queen if you don't like this one?'

Gerda shook her head firmly. 'I think your Snow Queen is much better than the one in the book!'

she said supportively. 'The one in the book is too scary – it would put me off my chess game. Why don't we read the story that goes with this picture?'

'I'll read it to you!' volunteered Kai, happily. 'It's called *A Mirror and its Pieces*.'

It was an odd story. It was about a hobgoblin who made a magic mirror. Anything seen reflected in this mirror looked ugly and hateful. The mirror would show people their ideas and wishes and dreams, but it would twist and distort them into something horrible and spoiled. The Hobgoblin thought this was an excellent piece of mischief, and had the idea of taking the mirror to the royal palace, to get the King and his court to look in it, and to make fools of them all. But as he flew to the palace carrying the mirror, he could not resist looking into it himself. The mirror shattered, and the pieces rained down everywhere.

'That's the scene in the picture of course,' Kai said, 'and here comes the bit about the Snow Queen – listen to this!'

And he read:

'But now the shattered mirror caused new kinds of misery. For, you see, every little piece of it had the power of the whole mirror. From time to time, a person would get a fragment of the glass in his eye, and then everything he looked at seemed joyless and horrid. And it was worse still if you got a fragment in your heart. Then your heart became cold, and you could no longer care for anybody or anything else, or mind whether you hurt them. That is what happened to the Snow Queen, the proud, free spirit of the frozen North. When her heart froze, she became a monster: gathering the mirror pieces and putting them into the eyes or hearts of people, turning these poor wretches into tools for her own cold-hearted plans. She no longer cared what harm she did to anyone.

At all this, the Hobgoblin laughed and laughed. Not only was it amusing – or so he thought – that the Snow Queen did his work for him. Better still, she did it so very well! For, although he delighted in causing trouble of every kind, the Hobgoblin was really very lazy. But as the Snow Queen was as cunning as an arctic fox, and as strong as a polar bear. She was as hard and relentless and bitter as the winter itself. And so the mirror did more harm than the Hobgoblin had ever dreamed.

I expect you are wondering whether the Hobgoblin's mischief could ever be undone, and so I will tell you now how someone tried to put things right.'

Kai turned the page, then some more pages. He looked baffled.

'That's all there is!' he said exasperatedly. 'There must be some pages missing. That's really annoying. I want to know how the story ends!'

'You can ask the storyteller about it when we see her,' replied Gerda. 'But please don't be cross about it now. It's so pleasant out here in the afternoon sunshine. I wish things could be just like this forever.'

'But it will be getting cold soon,' said Kai, practically.

Kai was right. A surprisingly cool northerly breeze was blowing down past the storyteller's tent when they visited the carnival that evening, as if autumn might come sooner than you'd expect. They arrived just as a show had ended and they fought against a current of excited customers spilling out of the tent.

'Ah!' said the storyteller, as she recognized Kai. 'Here's that clever boy who is so interested in the Snow Queen!'

She gave Kai a smile, but Gerda noticed that the smile didn't reach her eyes.

'And here's the Birthday Girl!' said the storyteller. 'Do you like the Snow Queen too?'

She offered a handshake, but the moment they touched hands, Gerda felt a sort of shock: a very unpleasant feeling of a connection of some kind. The storyteller snatched her hand back and her eyes became wary; she had felt it too.

'I suppose the Snow Queen is not to everyone's taste!' said the storyteller quickly to Gerda. 'But now then, young man, what did you think of that book, eh?'

'It's a lovely book, but there are some pages missing!' said Kai. He showed her. 'Look, this story can't possibly end here. We were wondering whether you know the end of *A Mirror and its Pieces*?'

'That one, eh?' said the storyteller softly. *Why is she giving Kai that intent look?* thought Gerda, uneasily.

'Not many people know that story beyond what you saw written down,' the storyteller said slowly after a moment. 'But I think I could ... '

Just then a large party of excited customers came in, ready for the next storytelling show. The storyteller seemed suddenly to change her mind.

'It's not a story for happy crowds, that one!' she said briskly. 'Why don't you stay for this show, and then we'll have a private telling later?'

'There are some other things I want to see,' said Gerda, firmly, feeling that somehow it was really important to get away.

Kai looked uncertainly from Gerda to the storyteller and back. 'Here's your book back,' he said.

'We'll come back in a while.' But Gerda was already pulling him firmly by the hand, out of the tent, determined not to return.

Gerda thought the best thing would be to distract Kai. They went around other stalls in as bright a whirl of enthusiasm as Gerda could manage. But it was no good. In the end they quarrelled, and Kai went back to the storyteller by himself.

Gerda sat alone, miserably, at the edge of the carnival, waiting at the place where they'd argued. She had stopped being angry with Kai now. Perhaps he was right after all – she had been feeling strange today: flashes of anger, worry, jealousy, unkindness, dread even. What was getting into her? With a bit of luck, Kai had gone back to the storyteller, heard the story, and would soon come to find her. Then they could be friends again.

She waited a long while. It was no good, she would have to go and find him.

The storyteller's tent was shut up for the night, with a hastily written note to say that further shows had been cancelled. There was no sign of the storyteller – or of Kai. Maybe Kai had heard the story and then gone home? She ran home, but Kai's family were surprised to see her – he had not come back.

Now they were all alarmed. Both families – Gerda's and Kai's – came back to the carnival to look. The carnival people joined in too. But it was only late in the evening that Kai was found. Gerda pushed her way to the front of the crowd as he was being lifted out of a ditch.

'He's alive!' someone said. But he was injured. There was a big bruise on the side of his head, and he had a black eye. As they lifted him onto a handcart to take him home, Gerda saw a tiny spot of blood on his white shirt, just over his heart. She cried out, and someone pulled Kai's shirt open to see, but there was no mark on his skin.

They brought Kai home. The doctor reassured them that not much seemed to be wrong, but they would have to wait to be sure. They waited.

Gerda was distraught, and barely comforted

by the arrival the next day of her favourite uncle, Anders. Uncle Anders went to see Kai. He spoke to the doctor. He came back to Gerda, looking thoughtful.

'Come,' he said to Gerda. 'As we must wait, let's pass the time as best we can. It's still summer, and since my ship did not quite arrive in time for your birthday ... ' (Uncle Anders was a sailor) ' ... I demand a special Gerda's birthday all of my own. So let me take you for a picnic up the hill. That will be a good place to have your present.'

So off they set. The walk was fine, Uncle Anders had even funnier stories than usual, and Gerda could almost forget her worries about Kai for a time. From where they sat picnicking at the edge of the woods, they could see all over the town.

'And now, you will see why I wanted to come to this spot before I gave you your present,' said Uncle Anders. He pulled a beautiful long, thin box from his pocket. It was a small telescope.

Gerda thanked him, and trained it on the town to try it out. There was their house, the balcony

leaping close through the
telescope and, as she
focused, there was ...

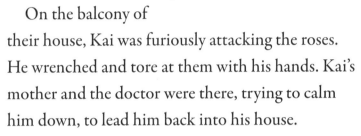

'Kai!' Gerda
shouted. 'But ... what
is he doing? No!'

On the balcony of
their house, Kai was furiously attacking the roses.
He wrenched and tore at them with his hands. Kai's
mother and the doctor were there, trying to calm
him down, to lead him back into his house.

Gerda lowered the telescope and stood
dumbfounded, mind reeling. Uncle Anders gently
took the telescope from her. He looked through it
himself. Then he sighed.

'You know, Gerda,' he said carefully, 'a bang on the
head, or a bad shock, can sometimes make people ...
not be themselves for a while. Try not to blame him.
The real, old Kai will be there inside, somewhere, I
know it. Try to be brave and patient while the real
Kai is away, just as you are patient when I am away.
Can you do that for me?'

'Can you do that for me?' was their game. Ever since she was a little girl, Uncle Anders would take leave of their family by looking teasingly at Gerda's father, then saying to Gerda, 'So, Gerda, I need you to look after my little brother while I'm away. He gets into all kinds of trouble – can you do that for me?' And usually Gerda would laugh and salute and say, 'Aye aye sir!' But this time she only nodded miserably.

Uncle Anders put a comforting arm around her shoulder and they walked home slowly, talking. By the time they reached their door, it was evening. Someone had taken the roses away. For the first time in years, the gate to Kai's balcony was shut. Only a few stray rose petals remained, swirling unwanted in the chill evening breeze.

They told Gerda not to try to see Kai yet, to be patient, and wait for him to get better. But she had waited, and waited; and now she stood alone on their balcony looking out at the winter snow. Last year, Kai would have been excitedly thumping on her door, wanting her to come sledging. This year ...

A door banged at street level, and Kai trudged off alone, dragging his sledge. *Hah*! Angry at last, Gerda yanked on her boots and coat and marched out after him.

She caught up with him at the top of the hill. She stopped, uncertain. Kai was standing by an ornate white sleigh. He was talking animatedly to the driver. Gerda could not hear him but she could see his face as he looked up towards the sleigh driver. His face was oddly blank. The driver – a bundle of white furs from where Gerda stood – nodded and gestured. To Gerda's horror, Kai climbed into the sleigh. The driver whipped up the horses, and they set off briskly downhill.

Gerda ran a few steps. No – pursuit was hopeless on foot. But the bumping of Uncle Anders' telescope in her pocket gave her a new idea.

The sleigh and its driver leaped into focus. The driver turned, and Gerda gasped. The driver looked

like the storyteller, but looked even more like ...
more like the Snow Queen.

Just for a moment Kai twisted round, looked
right back at Gerda through the telescope, and his
eyes screamed, 'Help me, Gerda!' as clear as could
be, even while the rest of his face showed only that
awful, unnatural blankness ...

Gerda was certain Kai had known she was there, that he had seen her at last, but it was too late now. Too late, because the sleigh had driven straight onto the frozen river at full speed. It skittered, then, with a monstrous sound, the ice cracked open like a vast jagged mouth. A tongue of water lolled out and licked back, and the sleigh and the driver and Kai were all swallowed by the river, and everything was lost.

When Gerda reached the bank with other would-be rescuers, there was nothing there: nobody struggling to the surface, nothing floating up. There was nothing when they broke the ice and groped with long poles. There was nothing, nothing, no trace at all – only muttering, baffled rescuers, and the river mutely icing over again like a wound healing, freezing like the tears on Gerda's face.

How could there be ... just nothing left at all?

Gerda was finally coaxed home, exhausted, chilled and unwell. She was carried off to bed, shivering.

In the deepest dark of the night she dreamed that she was lying in the snow. Someone was trying to get her to move, to walk to shelter. But she didn't want to. She was too tired and cold. It would be so much easier not to care any more, to stay in the snow.

Then she was bending over Kai, and Kai was unconscious in the snow, but as she looked down, his eyes opened. Kai looked at her, chilled half to death, and terrified.

The dream shifted again. Gerda and Kai rode in a carriage – or perhaps the carriage was flying. It was night. Wolves howled and a bright moon shone down. Flickering feathers of light began to flash in the sky – the Northern Lights rolling like brightly coloured waves. Then the carriage turned and the window went dark. As she turned her head to the window, Gerda knew that she didn't want to see her reflection. She struggled, but couldn't stop herself turning her head; in the darkened carriage window, the Snow Queen's face gazed back at her, with a look of cold satisfaction that was nothing like the panic Gerda felt inside. Gerda struggled to escape. There was a red flash and a noise, and Gerda started from sleep with a great gasp.

Someone had drawn back the curtains – it was morning. There were doctors, and worried faces looking at her. It was some time before she was well again.

2 The Woman Who Could Do Magic

Spring came, the snow thawed, and the ice of the frozen river broke up and floated away. It was a joyless spring for Gerda, bringing no relief from a bleak winter. She found herself often going down to the place where Kai had plunged into the river, sitting on a large stone near the bank, and watching the pieces of ice being swept away on the strong spring-flood current.

One day, Gerda arrived to find an old lady sitting on the stone in the spring sunshine. The snow was going now, and flowers were beginning to appear. The old woman turned her head and smiled at Gerda. Gerda tried not to stare rudely: the woman was blind in one eye. One eye was lively and brown but the other looked like a smoothed snowball.

The old woman slid herself across the stone a little, and patted the part where she had made a space. 'Come, my dear,' she said. 'There's room for two.' Gerda hesitated, then sat. The woman smiled and then went back to watching the river.

'I've seen you come here often this spring,' she said. 'Was this where that young man was pulled into the river by the runaway sleigh?'

Gerda nodded.

'But not a hair, or a spar of wreckage did they ever find,' the old lady continued. 'Makes you wonder what happened to him, doesn't it?' She looked piercingly at Gerda, her good eye searching Gerda's face.

'He ... he was my best friend,' Gerda ventured. 'Everyone thinks he drowned.'

The old lady looked sceptical, and turned back to watch the river.

'Drowned, but no body? Crashed and no wreckage? Hmmm – I wonder what the river would say, if you could ask it?' She turned to Gerda again.

'You want to ask the river, don't you? That's why you keep coming here, looking for answers.'

'Do you think Kai might still be alive?' asked Gerda, standing up in sudden agitation.

'Well ... *I* don't know,' said the old lady, gruffly. 'The river might know, if you cared to ask it.'

And she turned back to the river, watching it again and nodding her head.

'I'd give anything to find Kai!' said Gerda, fervently.

'Would you, now?' said the old lady, turning her head to Gerda again. 'But children want a great many things that they don't want to give payment for. Would you give those lovely red shoes you are wearing?'

'Of course!' exclaimed Gerda – it seemed like a silly question. 'If Kai is alive, we must find him! If he's dead, then ... then at least we will have him to bury.' She already had one red shoe in her hand, as if she really could exchange the shoes for news of Kai.

The old lady looked at her thoughtfully.

'Well then,' she said, 'I believe that might do. And how do you think you might ask the river?'

Gerda found herself shouting, 'Where is Kai?' She flung the shoe into the water. At the splash, a startled crow flew up from its tree.

'WHERE IS KAI?' Gerda shouted again, ripping off the second shoe and hurling it into the river to join the first.

'Very good, very good!' said the old woman. 'But watch now – let us see what the river says.'

The shoes had come together in the current. They swirled for a moment and then they were cast up together on a large piece of ice that was still stuck fast to the shady north bank.

'Kai would say that I didn't throw the shoes in far enough,' said Gerda quietly. She was beginning to feel silly, and icy mud was squelching up around her stockinged feet. She sat down heavily and forced back a sob.

'Hah!' said the old woman, unimpressed. 'Young people today! You think far too much and look and feel far too little. But what do *you* think, my dear?'

Gerda looked at the shoes for a long moment, then jumped up with a sudden conviction. 'Kai is alive!' she said excitedly.

'Very good indeed!' said the old lady, now watching Gerda intently. 'And what—'

'Kai is alive, and he's in the icy Far North!' said Gerda again, suddenly sure of it, though Kai would have said this made no sense.

The old woman looked at her in surprise for a moment. Then she clapped her hands. 'Excellent, excellent: so he is! And of course, you were saying that if he were alive, you would have to go and find him. Come, come, I can start you on your way!' She sprang up without any signs of stiffness, took Gerda

by the hand, and led her briskly a little
way upstream.

'Yes, yes, come along!' she said impatiently,
pulling a small boat into the bank, and ushering
Gerda into it. Then she got into the boat, cast
off, and let the current take them. They quickly
rounded the bend of the river and were away
downstream. For a while, a crow wheeled above
them, but the swift little boat soon left it behind.

'You will be hungry, I expect,' said the old woman a while later. 'Cold, too. Untie that bundle – you'll find a warm shawl, some boots and something nice to eat.'

Gerda rummaged. The boots were good, and exactly her size. The shawl was soft, fine wool. Once again, she hadn't realized how cold she'd become. There was a box of cherries – the first fresh fruit Gerda had seen this year, so early in the spring – and a flask of water.

Gerda took a cherry. It was delicious, like spring and summer and sunshine. It was a long time since Gerda had enjoyed food. In a moment, she was eating the cherries greedily, with an urgency that matched the rushing spring-flood of water all around them.

'Good, good, do eat them all,' the old lady said with satisfaction, without looking around from her paddling. 'I have many more at my house, and that's where we'll go ... to start with.'

Gerda put the empty cherry box down. She felt so sleepy that she curled up in the bottom of the boat, unable to keep her eyes open a moment longer. She slept. The old woman at last looked round with a smile. It wasn't a simple, kind smile: there was triumph in it too. Then she turned back to her paddling once more. The river was treacherous this early in the spring and they had far to go if they were to reach her house before Gerda woke.

Gerda awoke, and for a moment she had no idea where she was. She sat up in the bed with a start. 'Of course,' she said to herself. 'I am in my bedroom in Granny's house. I've always been living with Granny. I help her in her garden.' It sounded right, but somehow it felt just a bit wrong.

She slipped out of bed, and put on her clothes. 'It's the best flower garden in the world,' she continued to herself. 'There's not a flower that we don't grow.' And again, that felt just slightly wrong. Wasn't she thinking, only last week, that there was

a flower she knew from somewhere, which she
couldn't find in the garden? But Granny had said
that was just a dream.

It was another beautiful late summer's day.
Granny was doubtless already out in her garden.
But she would have left some breakfast in
the kitchen for Gerda – there would
definitely be some cherries! There
were always cherries – and
Granny was always so
eager for Gerda
to eat them!

There was a noise as Gerda came into the kitchen. She laughed – a crow had flown in through the open window, and was sitting on the windowsill, next to the usual bowl of cherries. As Gerda watched, it looked at her intelligently, tipped the bowl out of the window with a crash, then looked at her again. Gerda felt a moment of panic – she had to eat cherries every day! But that felt so very nonsensical that she stopped short. Why 'every day'? There were always plenty of cherries here. They weren't the rare treat they were at home ...

Gerda stopped. 'At home?' She suddenly realized that she couldn't remember any other place but here.

She opened the door and gently shooed the crow out. She followed it into the garden, fishing for memories of another place – somewhere with a balcony, with a person on the balcony. Things that were important to her somehow, but which were nothing to do with Granny.

Gerda stood in the sunny garden, feeling puzzled – and rebellious too. Why did she always do whatever Granny wanted, without question? Surely she had her own ideas and plans? Hadn't there been something really important she had to do? Something that involved ... a river, snow? Why couldn't she remember?

The crow watched her carefully, impressed. It fluttered around the corner and Gerda followed.

Around the corner, there was a sunny place and a garden seat, and a trellis that ran up the cottage wall, ready for some sun-loving, climbing plant. But the flower bed below it was empty – and that looked strange in a garden that was so thoroughly planted. Granny had been teaching her the thoughts of plants, and the wisdom of the earth. As Granny had taught her, she pushed her hand down into the soil to see what kind of plant it might like to grow. There was a plant already there! Getting to her knees, she scraped away some soil, and saw to her surprise that there weren't roots, as she had expected, but leaves and shoots. And there was a flower. Gerda thought she had not seen this kind of flower before, but at the same time she knew she had. She knew this plant well. It was important somehow.

'Who are you?' she asked the plant.

'You're not supposed to see me!' said the plant. It sounded nervous, but rebellious too. 'She says I'm to hide in the ground when you come by. And in all this lovely sunshine, too. It's cramped and stifling to be made to stay down here. It's not fair. It's cruel. And anyway, I've only got to hide so you don't remember ... ' It stopped abruptly, aware it had said far too much.

'Remember what?' asked Gerda. Then, more commandingly, 'Remember what?'

'I mustn't say ... I don't know!' said the plant, starting to panic.

'Very well,' said Gerda. She got to her feet, and brushed the soil from her knees. 'Come out so I can see you, but I won't make you tell me anything. The sunshine is truly lovely today,' she added, thinking of what Granny would do to get her way. 'And I know enough to command you, to make you come out anyway. Why not just come out now and enjoy the summer's day. There are bees ... '

It was too much, and with a creak, the plant uncoiled. Green shoots shot out of the ground and spiralled up into the trellis. Like years of growth all in a minute, the shoots hardened, grew woody and thorny. The plant sighed with relief. Flowers bloomed: red and scented and ... roses!

Roses! Gerda's mind reeled. Suddenly she remembered it all – her house and parents, Kai, the book, the storyteller, the shoes and the river. And the old lady who had tricked her into staying in this garden all summer, and had made her call her 'Granny' when she should be searching for Kai!

The rose gave a squeal of alarm.

'Oh dear,' said Granny, coming up behind. 'I am so sorry, my dear. I was so hoping to spare you all this. But I see you are already outgrowing my power.' She sounded more sad than angry.

'You ... tricked me,' growled Gerda, furious.

'It was for your own good!' protested the old lady.

'Listen child, it's quite clear that the Snow Queen has taken your friend. He's as good as dead: worse than dead, in fact! There isn't anything you can do. Once she has power over someone ... ' The old lady's hand strayed up to her blinded eye. 'Not many get away, and those that do pay a terrible price, believe me!' She put her hand on Gerda's arm. 'I've just been trying to keep you safe, my dear.'

'I don't want to be safe! I want to find Kai!' replied Gerda savagely, snatching her arm away.

'No good can come from going after him!' the old lady said firmly. 'And you've such talent, my dear, working out the river like that. And how quickly you've learned from me! You have power, young lady! And power is what the Snow Queen wants – don't let her catch you and take yours!'

The crow had fluttered onto the top of the trellis. The old lady looked at it suspiciously.

'You can't keep me here against my will!' said Gerda firmly.

'No,' replied the old lady, looking from the crow to Gerda and nodding slowly. 'No, I can't, can I?

Did your crow friend tell you that, or did you work it out for yourself?' Then suddenly she smiled at Gerda, and it seemed a genuine smile. 'You're a bold one!' she said. 'I used to be so bold, and I hope it wears better on you. Well, we will just have to see what your fate is to be.' She shot the crow a venomous look. 'So! I won't stop you from going, and I won't try to stop you again if you do get out, but I'm not going to help you, either. I warn you: the way out of my garden is hard to find, and perilous to travel. Let's see what you can do.'

And she sat down on the garden seat, folded her arms and looked at Gerda, waiting.

'Please do not be angry with this rose,' said Gerda, putting her hand on it. 'I made it come up.'

She realized something. 'I tempted and persuaded it against its will, and now I am sorry.'

The old woman gave a bitter little laugh. 'A bit of temptation and persuasion can get you a long way, you know.'

Gerda shook her head, turned to the rose and said to it, 'I need to leave the garden. Can you show me the way?'

The rose stirred, though there was no wind. Its branches pulled the trellis outwards like curtains opening. Behind, where the cottage wall should have been, a thicket of briars now stretched away into the gloom. A narrow, unwelcoming path curved away out of sight.

'Why not stay with Granny?' said the old lady, with one final appeal. Gerda ignored her and stepped into the thicket.

She seemed to be in a dense undergrowth of thorny plants. As she ventured deeper, there was barely enough light to see in the gloomy tangle. Gerda moved warily along the track. Thorny runners sprawled across the path, half-seen in the gloom and ready to trip or grasp at her. Soon she came to a place where tracks crossed. She stopped to consider. If the challenge was a maze of confusing choices, she must stick to a principle, not lose her head. Some of the thicket was certainly climbing roses, like the ones she and Kai knew so well from their balcony. But there was another plant too, one Gerda didn't know. It had bitter, hooked thorns and tortured, misshapen stems. These turned in on themselves as if they had long given up seeking the light and now only sought to block and ensnare. So each time Gerda came to a junction, she followed the path that had more roses. She grew more hopeful as she went. And, after a time, she turned a corner and saw the light streaming in at the end of the thicket.

Was this really all there was to escaping? She stepped out of the undergrowth, and, like the shift of a dream, she found herself in a beech wood. The light was shining down strongly, making the trees look almost gold. And indeed the leaves were beginning to turn, and a stray one spiralled down onto her shoulder. There was a bit of mist, or maybe smoke tumbling in the sunbeams. It was then that she heard someone humming.

3 A Princess and Her Plans

Sitting under the trees was a young man with jet black hair. As he hummed, he was using a penknife to carve something. As Gerda walked towards him she trod on a stick. There was a loud crack and he looked up.

'You're none too good at sneaking up on folks, are you?' he asked amiably.

'I'm sorry,' said Gerda. 'I didn't mean to startle you. I'm lost. Or at least, I'm trying to find someone and I don't know where to go next.'

'You're lost and you're trying to find someone?' laughed the man, looking at her with flickering eyes.

'Sounds like you need to sort yourself out first, before you're any use to anyone else!'

He stood up. 'Sorry, where's me manners? I'm Jack.' He held out a hand for Gerda to shake, then realized there was something black on it. 'Oops, boot polish! Just like you'd expect from the boot boy. But it comes in dead handy for this chess set I'm making.'

He seemed to have forgotten about shaking hands now and showed her the chess pieces.

'Mad for the old chess, is the Princess's new friend. They fished him out of the river last winter – at death's door, he was – and the first thing he did when he got better was to ask for a chess set. Taught Her Royal Highness to play and all. So, I'm thinking, if me and Rosalind – that's my sweetheart – give the Princess a nice chess set, it might do us well when we want to ask her about my promotion. So here I am on my day off whittling chessmen.' He looked up at the sky. 'It's getting a bit late now, though. I'd best be getting back. And if you're lost, as you say, I can't do no better than to take you to the palace. You'll find your way on from there all right.'

He gathered up his chessmen, and set off. Gerda fell into step with him. She could see a castle ahead in the valley, by a river. Evening was coming fast now – wisps of mist were already rising from the river and it was getting colder as they walked.

'As a matter of fact,' Gerda said cautiously, 'I'm looking for someone who fell into the river last winter. What did you say the Princess's friend looks like?'

'Well, let's see now,' said Jack. 'He's about your height – about the same age, I think. Blond where you're red-headed. Little scar over his right eye.'

Gerda stopped dead. It sounded just like Kai. 'And he was rescued from the river, you say?'

'Yes,' said Jack, 'back when it thawed up a little last winter. And I said to Rosalind ... '

'What is his name?' asked Gerda swiftly, before Jack could ramble on any more.

'Well, funny thing is, he doesn't remember,' said Jack, tapping himself on the head. 'Bang on the head, I expect. He didn't remember a thing when he first woke up. It's mostly come back now, but he's never been too sure of the name. Said he thought "Guy" sounded familiar, so that's what we call him.'

Gerda gave a small squeal. Jack looked at her in surprise for a moment.

'Oh, I see!' he said after a while. 'You think this boy we've found might be the one you're looking for. What's his name, this bloke you're trying to find?'

'It's Kai,' said Gerda, weakly.

'Well, sounds like "Guy", doesn't it?' continued Jack. 'Lucky chap, if you ask me – fallen on his feet here ... ' Jack chattered away, but Gerda stopped listening. *What if Kai had not only survived, but had found a new life that was better,* she thought anxiously? She'd always thought that she would find him and bring him back, but what would she do if he didn't want to come?

Jack's sweetheart, Rosalind, met them at the servants' entrance to the palace. *Even the servants in this palace were prettier and better dressed than she was,* thought Gerda glumly.

'Look what I found in the woods!' said Jack, dramatically. 'A fine, flame-haired maiden on a quest. She's looking for a friend of hers and she thinks it might be Guy. Can you take her to see Her Royal Highness?' At last, when Rosalind had understood Jack's rambling explanations, she kissed his cheek and then took a candle and beckoned for Gerda to follow her.

They set off down a passageway. It was narrow and plain. 'I was expecting the inside of the palace to be grander,' Gerda said.

Rosalind laughed. 'No, girl,' she said. 'We're not in the main parts of the palace – those are grand enough. But the fine folks, they don't want to see us servants scurrying around doing all the work. So we have our own ways round the castle, and every room has a servants' door as well as the fancy doors for the fancy folk.'

The mist seemed to have followed them inside, and was now a wispy fog up to knee height. Gerda shivered.

'Can't you keep the mist outside?' she asked.

Rosalind stopped and turned to her, raising her candle high. 'Mist? No, it's not mist, girl. Dreams, thoughts, worries, maybe. I don't see them, so I suppose they must be yours, eh? Jack did say you were lost.'

She turned and carried on briskly. Gerda had no chance to ask about that odd remark. The mist swirled up, and it seemed to bank up behind them, and pursue them along the passageway.

Gerda's thoughts were in a worse and worse whirl. With a great effort, she forced herself to think what to do. If Kai was truly happy with his new friends, she decided, she would do her best to be happy for him.

She would miss him dreadfully if he didn't want to come home, but all she would insist upon was that he send a letter back with her, so that his family would know he was alive and well. That much he surely owed them, no matter how above them all his life now was. That felt right, and knowing what to do brought a little calmness, as Rosalind knocked on a grand door. Gerda straightened her dress nervously and followed Rosalind in. The mist flowed in too. It seemed to be thinning. 'Your Royal Highness,' Rosalind began. There were two people in the room, playing chess: a young woman, and a boy. And the boy was not Kai.

Rosalind was talking, telling Gerda's story, but Gerda couldn't concentrate on what was being said. She couldn't decide whether to laugh in relief, or cry that a hope had been snatched away. It wasn't Kai. It wasn't Kai who had fallen on his feet so well that he might not want to know her any more. But that meant that Kai was still somewhere: dead or alive, or most likely a prisoner of the Snow Queen as the old lady had said. She still had to find him, if she could. And here was something else: the mists had disappeared. How had she thought that this warm, light castle was dark and chill?

The Princess jumped up with excitement when she heard Gerda's story.

'Oh, that's so exciting and romantic!' she exclaimed, clapping her hands together, and looking at Gerda with shining eyes. 'We have a ball on Saturday, and you shall tell your tale there, and everyone will think it's most wonderfully gothic. I'll get my seamstress to make you a fine gown: black I think – no, that will make you look like a widow – maybe dark grey, with enough lace that you don't look like a governess. And gloves, of course. And a design of roses, and mirrorwork. Yes, yes, that would be perfect. And I will get the hairdresser to attend to your hair. And I will write a song about your adventure, that I can sing after you've told it, and everyone will think it's most diverting.'

She prattled on about this and that party or event at which she would show Gerda off. At last Gerda said, 'Your Royal Highness is most kind. But I still have to find my friend and … '

'Yes, yes, duties!' said the Princess, dismissively. 'I'll have my guards turn out and search for him. They can look all over, and I will send messages to all the neighbouring kingdoms, and they can all be looking while we have fun. Isn't that delightful?'

Gerda wondered for a moment whether this would actually be better. The Princess could send grown-up messengers in all directions. What could she do on her own, and only a girl? But then she thought about the Princess's guards: people who didn't know or care about Kai, except for any reward they might get from finding him, and bringing him back to the palace. And would they brave the Snow Queen to find him, some lost boy who was just another one of the Princess's 'duties'? No, she had to do it herself. She had already spent too long waiting.

'Your Royal Highness is most kind,' Gerda said quickly. 'But I have already been delayed by a witch who tricked me, and I really feel I must travel on at once.'

'A witch?' the Princess squealed, and insisted that Gerda told her that part of the story. It put the

Princess into absolute raptures. The Princess's gush of excitement ended only when Guy, who had been listening rather sourly, pointed out that it was late, and that their guest was perhaps tired.

'Oh dear,' the Princess said. 'You're quite right! Rosalind will show you to a guest room now, and in the morning we'll have a proper talk about it all. Rosalind, one more thing, please.'

And she whispered to Rosalind, ineptly, loud enough that Gerda could actually hear, 'Lock her bedroom door.'

Rosalind led Gerda to the bedroom.

'So, you're going to make me a prisoner then?' said Gerda, in dismay.

'Well, girl,' Rosalind replied, 'I've got the one key to lock the one door. Whether that will make you a prisoner, I couldn't say.' And Gerda remembered that each room had a servants' door as well. She brightened.

'Here's your room, then,' Rosalind continued, showing Gerda in. 'I had Cook put you up some supper, as you'll probably be hungry'. She curtsied, and left. Gerda heard the key turn in the lock, then she was alone.

The supper did look delicious, and Gerda decided that escaping on a full stomach would be a much better plan. While she ate, she looked around. Finally, she saw the servants' door – concealed to look like part of a bookcase, but clear enough once you noticed it. She crossed to the bookcase, and opened the door. Then she stopped. Rosalind and Jack had been kind, and she didn't want them to get into trouble.

Gerda turned back to the writing desk in the room, and found paper, pen and ink.

'Your Royal Highness,' she wrote, 'I am sorry, but I really must continue with my quest, and so I cannot stay with you, no matter how delightful that would be. So I have used my magic to disappear from this room and travel far away. Yours sincerely, Gerda the Enchantress.'

Then she set off through the servants' door, and nearly bumped into Rosalind, who was coming along the passageway outside.

'That's the spirit, Miss,' said Rosalind, 'though if your courage will hold, you might do better to escape first thing in the morning when it's light, and easier to travel. I expect you could do with a good night's sleep, too.'

Gerda knew now that her courage would hold until morning. If she had briefly wavered, thought about leaving the Princess's men to find Kai, then that idea was long gone. She decided that Rosalind could be trusted. She smiled, went back into her room, and went to bed.

Gerda was already up the next morning when she heard Rosalind in the servants' passageway. Silently she went through the door, shut it carefully behind her and followed Rosalind through the castle, and along the gravel paths of the dewy morning garden. Gerda stole nervous glances back at the palace windows, but every last one was sleepily curtained. Nobody saw them as they made their way to a long arbour made by training roses up an iron arch. It made a green tunnel, with the last few flowers of the year still holding on.

They walked through the arbour and Rosalind put her hand on a gate at the far end. 'Here is the way out of the castle,' she said. 'I can go no further.'

'Will you get into trouble?' Gerda asked anxiously.

Rosalind laughed. 'I don't think so – you left by magic, remember? I'll take that message to the Princess, and she'll say "It's all so enchanting" and maybe she'll turn out the Guard to chase you, but they won't bother to look long or far. And more likely, she'll make a story and a song of you, and have as much fun as if you'd stayed. Well goodbye, Miss.

And good luck!'

Rosalind swung the gate open. But
Gerda gave a cry – there, on
the road, standing by a
little gypsy caravan, was
Granny. The crow was
perched on the roof.

Rosalind pulled Gerda
to her side. 'She has got
out,' Rosalind said angrily to
the old woman. 'You cannot
stop her again – you gave
your word in the garden. Both
rose and crow heard you.'

The old woman waved her hand impatiently. She
kept looking nervously at the crow. 'Of course I'm
not going to stop her. This whole business is clearly
too big for me, and I wish I hadn't got involved in
it. If you will believe it, dear,' she said, turning to
Gerda, 'I see I misjudged you. You have got out.
You're not put off by confusion, nor your fears, nor
temptations. Maybe you can find your friend after

all, and take the Snow Queen down a peg or two. I'd like that – she's no friend of mine. So I've decided to help.' She gestured at the caravan.

Rosalind looked suspicious. 'Are all these things only what they seem to be?' The crow nodded, and hopped onto the horse's head. The old lady looked at it sulkily.

'Well that's more than can be said for either of you!' she retorted, glowering at Rosalind and the crow. Then the old lady sighed. 'Well, I suppose it's nobody's fault but my own if people don't trust me,' she said to Gerda. 'But I really do feel I was wrong, and I do want to make amends. So, you see, I have a special gift for you. If you do find your friend, you may need it.' From a pocket she pulled out a locket on a chain necklace, and laid it on the driver's seat of the caravan. Gerda didn't move but the crow hopped onto it suspiciously, and pecked at it cautiously.

'Ha!' snorted the old lady, glowering at the crow, offended. 'Well, if you're all as suspicious as that, I won't tell you how it works!' She turned on her heel and strode off crossly down the road.

Despite everything, Gerda felt just a bit sorry for her. 'Goodbye, Granny!' she called. The old woman raised a hand in acknowledgement, but she didn't stop marching away, and she didn't look around.

The crow, satisfied with the locket now, pushed it towards Gerda with its beak. Gerda stepped forward and took it, but put it in a pocket rather than trying it on, just in case. She ran back and hugged Rosalind. Then she quickly took stock of the caravan. There was a bundle inside – good sensible outdoor clothes, food, water, and other things for a journey. Anxious to get some distance between herself and any pursuit, she set the horse off down the road heading north, and had a breakfast of bread and cheese while she drove. For a while the crow flew alongside, then she lost sight of it.

4 The Robbers and a Girl

It all happened so fast. The robbers were swift and skilful, and gave Gerda no chance. One moment the horse was plodding quietly along the road; the next, masked figures appeared as if by magic from out of the trees. One grabbed the reins, and another leaped up onto the driver's seat and forced Gerda down the steps. A third robber tied her to a tree while the others ransacked the caravan.

Gerda tried to look braver than she felt as she was being tied up. She looked into the merciless icy blue eyes above the scarf concealing the robber's face. She wondered for a moment if she could struggle free and run. But there were too many of them – escape was hopeless.

Another robber, larger and older, came over to look at Gerda. 'Well, not much for us here, is there?' the older robber said. 'Horse and cart, clothes and food, and just you, all by yourself. Travelled some days on your own, by the look of it.' He nodded and seemed to have decided something.

'Take the horse and cart,' he called out to his men.
'Leave the girl tied up.'

'No, she's my prisoner,' said the blue-eyed robber,
in an odd toneless voice. 'And I'll take the
clothes, too.'

That seemed to settle it. The other robbers
seemed wary of the blue-eyed one, a little afraid,
even. Once they reached the camp, the main party
of robbers took Gerda's caravan off in one direction,
but the blue-eyed robber led Gerda a little further
into the woods to a neat little encampment set on
its own, and tied her carefully to one of the trees,
near a small campfire.

'Now we will tell stories around the campfire,'
announced the robber, taking off the hat and scarf.
Gerda suddenly realized that her captor was a girl,
only a little older than Gerda herself.

'The men are going to have a party tonight, but
they're stupid and annoying. So we shall have our
own party. You shall tell the first story.'

The only plan Gerda could think of was to tell her
own tale. Maybe, if she could keep this strange girl

talking, there would be a chance for her to escape. She had just got to the Hobgoblin's mirror when a small, terrified boy came through the trees with two plates of food.

'This is Beorn,' said the robber girl. 'Beorn will dance when I twist his arm behind his back. It's not a very good dance, but I think he might get better if I make him practise. And perhaps I need to twist his arm harder. Shall I make him dance now?'

'No!' said Gerda. 'I mean, I'm in the middle of the story – don't you want to hear the rest?' Beorn shot her a grateful glance and fled. Gerda went back to the story. The robber girl began to eat, and after a moment decided to untie Gerda so that she could eat too.

Once the story was over, the robber girl said, 'Now I shall look at the things I have stolen from you.'

She rummaged through Gerda's clothes. Then she found the locket that the old woman had given Gerda. She found how to open the locket, and checked carefully to see if it was really empty.

But the moment the robber girl fastened the locket around her neck, her face contorted in pain.

She clutched her chest and fell to her knees. She seemed to be dying. Gerda was torn between two wild impulses – to take this chance to escape on the one hand, or to try and help the dying girl.

It was no good – Gerda couldn't leave the robber girl in agony. But as she laid a hand on the girl's shoulder, the girl straightened and looked up. In her hands she was holding the locket, and it was open. Inside it was something shiny – a dagger-shaped shard of mirror which flashed flame in the campfire light. A single drop of blood was staining her shirt over her heart. The girl looked at Gerda in bemusement for a moment, then suddenly flung herself at Gerda and hugged her.

'You've cured me! From the mirror shard! How did you know?' the girl cried, her voice warm and excited, and very unlike the blank monotone of before. 'Oh!' she said suddenly, looking crestfallenly at the locket. 'This will have been for curing your friend Kai. I hope I haven't spoiled things by using it already.'

'I ... ' started Gerda. 'I think you should keep the

locket. I'm glad I could help and … '

She thought a moment, smiled and added truthfully, 'I would never have found out what it did without you.'

It wasn't this girl's fault, Gerda thought. And maybe the locket could work twice? If not, she would find another way to save Kai. Surely she would. She had to.

'I'm so, so sorry!' the other girl carried on. 'I can't believe the things I've been doing with that mirror splinter in my heart. It's … awful … ' Her voice trailed off and she looked appalled. Then she burst into tears.

Gerda found herself comforting her captor and robber. 'You couldn't help what happened,' she said reasonably. 'All you can do is to try and do the right things now.'

The other girl forced herself to calm down.

'You're right,' she said, composing herself with a sniff. 'I must do what I can to make amends. I'll start by getting you out of this wretched robber camp. And I'll need to get myself out too. Can I come with you? I'm no longer heartless, thanks to you, but I'm practical and tough. I can guide you through the land hereabouts, and I know how to live in these woods. Will you take me along?'

'I would love to have you,' said Gerda sincerely. And her tough, practical companion broke down into tears of gratitude on her shoulder once more. Then she gave a small giggle.

'Robbers have no manners at all!' she said with a smile and a mock-formal curtsey. 'I'm Frida, and I am truly pleased to meet you!'

5　A Wise Woman in the Snow

Gerda and Frida slipped quietly away from the robbers' camp in the clammy early morning. The camp was not stirring at all. The robbers had stayed up late the night before, and were soundly asleep.

They left on foot – the robbers would certainly come after them if they took Gerda's horse and caravan. But Frida realized now that the robbers would probably be glad she was leaving. They had been afraid of her in her heartless state, and had allowed her to stay only because she was useful in her ruthlessness. They wouldn't waste time hunting the two girls, if they left without stealing anything. Frida had all that they really needed from her own little camp, including a small bag of money. In the strengthening morning light, Gerda realized that Frida's eyes were a soft grey, and no longer the chill blue of yesterday.

For several days, Frida led them north. Looking back later in her life, Gerda remembered it as a good time. The weather stayed fine, and Frida was the ideal companion, with a thousand skills to find the way, to find a place to make a camp at night, to collect nuts and berries and other foods from the autumn woods, and to hunt with a slingshot. At night, the girls huddled under a great cloak for warmth, and took turns to stay awake on watch.

Frida's sleep was troubled by nightmares, and Gerda would stay close and stroke her friend's hair to comfort her. But one morning, Gerda's comfortable dream was stirred by a cold draught; her dream turned dark and cold and she dreamt she was standing in the snow. The wind howled and the clouds streamed towards her, torn before the wind. They flushed red in the sunset and dispersed, replaced by clouds of green and sky-blue flame that streamed and swarmed.

In the dream, the Snow Queen was cowering at Gerda's feet. Gerda was huge, mighty in her righteousness, and swollen with revenge. She screeched at her enemy, and the Northern Lights writhed red with her rage, arcing down like miles-broad lightning, blasting the ground where her rival was. Gerda's anger flashed and arced down the lights, surging, on and on. The power was at once awful and ecstatic. Then the lights turned green, an unnatural chemical green, then pale blue and she was being drained, drained, but could not stop. She hadn't meant to do this – only to rescue Kai and go. But she couldn't stop the lights.

At last it stopped. It was cold. She was freezing to her very heart. But where was Kai, or Frida, or the Snow Queen? The lights flared up into the huge shape of the Hobgoblin, holding his mirror. He made her look into the mirror – where she didn't want to look – to see herself as the new Snow Queen, her love and her hate frozen together into a bleak, blank wasteland.

The Hobgoblin laughed uproariously. The mirror crazed, spidering into a web of cracks. Then it exploded in her face.

Gerda woke with a start – but it was snow, not

glass or blood that was making her face wet. She felt sick. The colours of the Northern Lights swirled and danced in the middle of her pounding head. The pattern of the cracked mirror floated in her vision and for a moment she thought it was too late – she had a mirror shard in her eye! But she could see her friend Frida clearly through the flashes and cracks in her vision, and she loved Frida, so it was all right – she could still feel.

They were in the woods, of course. She was huddled under their cloak, but Frida had got up to look at the glowering gunmetal-dark clouds. Flurries of snow were beginning to fall, gusting on a bleak wind from the north. The whiteness and the cold and the swirling hurt Gerda's head. She stood with difficulty and supported herself against the rough bark of a silver birch. She could feel the life in it and its patient wait for spring, and this steadied her.

'I don't like this!' Frida said, looking out at the clouds. 'There's an unnatural lot of snow up there for autumn.' Then she turned, started, and hastened to Gerda's side in alarm.

'Headache,' explained Gerda with difficulty. 'Bad dream. Bit sick. But all right soon. We should go ... '

She took a deep, shaky breath and slowly lifted her stiff neck to look up, and met the eyes of a crow looking intently down from a low branch.

'Frida ...' said Gerda decisively after a moment, 'we have to follow this crow.'

Frida struck camp as swiftly as she could and they set off. The pewter-grey clouds loomed up closer, blown in by the chill north wind. Then the snow began to fall heavily. Soon they found that they were battling into the strong headwind, and that it was forcing its icy way into their clothes.

Frida led them off the road into the woods alongside. It would be slower going, but much more sheltered, she explained cheerfully. Gerda toiled along, miserably. Frida insisted on rests every hour or so. She dug out the dried fruit they'd taken from her camp, and they both ate some. She tried to make a game of the fruit they had to eat, and have them eat it along to a song. Gerda found herself beginning to grumble. It seemed that she could hear her voice complaining, without her having the energy to stop it or be at all kind, or nice, or reasonable. She was colder than cold– the snow was beginning to soak through her clothes. She didn't want to eat the fruit, and Frida's game was stupid. And why did Frida keep asking her questions, and slipping a hand into Gerda's hood to feel her neck? And why did she have to wrap a scarf over her nose and mouth? Why was Frida making such a fuss? Why couldn't she just leave her alone? Gerda was too lost in her own misery to see the concern in Frida's eyes, as Frida looked around more and more urgently for somewhere to take shelter.

'Look, Frida,' said Gerda absently after a long while. 'There's the crow again.'

Frida turned, and saw that Gerda had lagged behind once more. Not only that, but she had thrown back her hood, and taken the scarf off her face again. Her hair was bedraggled with sleet and dripping freezing water down inside her cloak. But she no longer seemed to care.

Frida hastened back to her. 'That's right, Gerda! The crow!' she said as cheerfully as she could, quietly rearranging Gerda's hood and scarf and tightening her cloak for her. Gerda didn't resist now.

She felt icy. 'Come on, Gerda!' Frida carried on brightly. 'Let's follow the crow! The crow has helped you before. Maybe it's come to help again.'

Did the crow nod, Frida wondered, or was the cold getting to her too? Anyway, it was in the direction she thought they should go, a village she'd been to once, where they might find shelter. And this new idea got Gerda moving once more, though with a bit of a stagger. The crow flapped ahead, but not too far, as if it did intend them to follow.

'Have you come to help? Please help!' Frida said to it silently. 'My friend can't last much longer. She'll collapse soon, and I'm too weak to carry her.'

Gerda staggered along after the crow. But she had forgotten why. She couldn't feel her feet. She could hear, but no longer understand, Frida talking as they followed the crow out into a small clearing, along the line of a paddock fence, and saw a cottage. They could see the door. But Gerda at last could go not a step further. She fell, and in a daze, she dreamed that she was lying in the snow. Someone was trying to get her to move, to walk the last little way to shelter. But she didn't want to – she was too tired and cold. It would be so much easier not to care any more, to stay in the snow forever ...

Gerda came to because she was shivering so much. She had blankets wrapped around her – someone must have taken off her soaked travelling clothes and wrapped her in these. She was in an armchair by a warm fire. Frida (in another armchair on the other side of the fire, and also wrapped in blankets) was grinning at her.

Frida was sipping a hot drink which smelled delicious. Her bare foot stuck out from her blankets, and she was wiggling her toes contentedly in the warm air by the fire.

'She's awake, Mrs Lappekonen,' Frida called, and a kindly-looking woman came into view from around the back of Gerda's armchair.

'Hello, Gerda dear,' said Mrs Lappekonen. She looked Gerda over, felt her neck, and then pulled another blanket from a pile and wrapped it around her. Gerda tried and failed to speak through her chattering teeth.

'The shivering is good,' Mrs Lappekonen said. 'No fun, I'm sure, but it means you're warming up. Are your toes and fingers hurting?' Gerda nodded. Mrs Lappekonen looked at Gerda's hands and feet.

'Well, that's another good sign – you're not going to lose them. I think we might try another blanket, and some soup as soon as you stop shaking.' She went out of sight – probably to get the soup.

'Where are we?' Gerda asked Frida, as soon as she'd got her chattering teeth under control.

'Mrs Lappekonen's house. She is someone who tried to help me once ... before,' said Frida. She looked at the fire for a moment, then turned back to Gerda, her eyes bright with tears.

'It's all right,' said Gerda. 'You don't need to tell me if it's painful.'

Frida nodded. 'Oh, Gerda! I'm so glad to see you awake. I was afraid that I'd lose the first friend I've made in so long!'

'I would have died in the snow without you,' said Gerda simply, only now realizing how close it had been. She reached out and squeezed Frida's hand. Then Mrs Lappekonen came back with two big bowls of hot soup. She handed one to Frida, but insisted on feeding Gerda spoonful by hot, delicious spoonful, pausing when Gerda broke into shivering fits. The shivering grew less, and a warm drowsiness – but a healthy one – crept over Gerda. At length, soup finished and shivering ceased, she went back to sleep.

The snow was still falling, but for days a freezing wind had battered the little cottage and at last that had stopped.

'You should be able to travel again tomorrow, if you want to,' said Mrs Lappekonen. 'Now, I expect you're anxious to know how your friend Kai is? Come look in the fire and see!'

The three of them crouched by the fire. For a

while Gerda saw only the fire.
Then she suddenly seemed
to see beyond the flames
and through the flames.
Kai sat on an
ice-blue throne, in a
palace made of packed
snow. He himself
was pale white, nearly
blue. He was working
on some sort of puzzle – pieces of glass or
mirror in an ornate frame. He moved the pieces
into combination after permutation, as if he was
trying to organize them in some meaningful way.
His fingers moved swiftly and deftly, but his face
was blank.

'If he can only complete the puzzle, he will be
free,' said Mrs Lappekonen quietly. 'In some part of
his soul he still knows that. But he cannot see clearly
because of the mirror splinter the Snow Queen has
put in his eye. The puzzle probably looks like the
most beautiful thing in the world to him, and that

keeps him working, but he will never do it unaided. You mustn't worry that he is suffering. His heart has been nearly frozen by the Snow Queen, and he only knows the puzzle. Some day, the ice will conquer his heart completely, and he will stop working altogether. There's many a statue in the Snow Queen's palace. Kai has held on surprisingly well – many of the Snow Queen's victims would have been frozen through long before. His heart must be hard to freeze!'

'Maybe his heart already belongs to someone else,' came Frida's voice. Gerda blushed deeply, and in that moment the vision faded.

'In the morning, you can rescue him,' said Mrs Lappekonen.

'Will you come with us?' asked Frida. Mrs Lappekonen shook her head. 'I cannot enter the Snow Queen's fortress without her knowing it immediately, even though she is not there herself at the moment. But because the Snow Queen is not at home, with any luck the two of you can get in, rescue Kai and bring me that puzzle, all before she knows about it. I can help you to the last ridge before her castle. But I can give you no greater power than Gerda already has – and you must have learned, in all your adventures, how very strong that is.'

Gerda nodded nervously. 'Yes, I am strong,' she said. 'That's one of the things that worries me. I keep dreaming that I am the Snow Queen myself. The night before you found us, Mrs Lappekonen, I dreamt that I fought the Snow Queen, only to become a new Snow Queen. That was why I was so shaken, Frida.'

Mrs Lappekonen moved to crouch down in front of Gerda and looked in her eyes for a long moment.

'You are right,' she said with a sigh. 'You could challenge her. But your dream has told you that you must not. We are shaped by the things we do, Gerda. You cannot use the Snow Queen's methods without risking becoming like her. That would be a disaster – you'd be a far stronger queen than the one you replaced. That, of course, is the other reason I cannot come too. I must not challenge her either. But Frida may help you, Gerda, if she will.'

'Of course I will,' said Frida. 'Gerda saved me! I know what it's like to be in the Snow Queen's power. Of course I want to save Kai from that.'

'I'm glad you will be there, Frida,' Mrs Lappekonen said. 'I do feel that you have something Gerda needs very much. You will know what it is when the time comes.'

'When I became the Snow Queen in my dream,' said Gerda slowly, 'I had this feeling that I couldn't help it, that it was my fate.' She turned a worried face to Mrs Lappekonen, who shook her head.

'If I thought you were going to become the next Snow Queen, of course I would not let you go. But Her current frozen Majesty is far away and will stay that way, I hope. Now go to bed, both of you, and sleep well, and do not worry. In the morning, I have something to show you, to help you on your journey.'

The next morning, Mrs Lappekonen found them warm cloaks and boots and led them outside.

In Mrs Lappekonen's paddock stood a brown reindeer with massive antlers, who was contentedly chewing a pile of parsnips. It exuded a sense of raw power. Gerda had never seen an animal so big, so alive. He trotted towards them. He towered over the girls, and had to lower his great head to nuzzle Gerda's glove.

'This is Ba,' said Mrs Lappekonen. 'He'll take you to the Snow Queen's palace, if you truly want to go.'

They were to ride Ba (to Gerda's thrilled delight), but would not need a saddle or reins. 'If Ba wants you to ride him, he keeps you on,' said Mrs Lappekonen. 'You can hold on to his antlers if you're nervous, but really I find the worst of it is trying not to fall asleep. And as for reins, well ... you don't need those.' Mrs Lappekonen laughed. 'Ba will go anywhere you want him to go, as long as he wants to go there himself, of course! Don't worry, Frida dear, Ba knows the way.'

They climbed up onto Ba's back: Frida in front, still not all that sure about riding bareback, and Gerda behind, clinging on to Frida more tightly than she realized. Ba's breath steamed in the still air.

Gerda tried to thank Mrs Lappekonen yet again, but the old lady waved it away with a smile. She swung the paddock gate open. Ba snorted, walked down to the far end of the field, then charged at the open gate. He gathered speed at a phenomenal rate. Gerda risked a brief wave to Mrs Lappekonen, before feeling she ought to cling on tight. Frida, sober-faced, held Ba's antlers. Mrs Lappekonen waved and called out as they shot past, then they were away.

After that huge surge, Ba's motion became as smooth as a boat on a stream. The world hurtled around them with a huge roar of wind. The falling snow rushed towards them in a blur. Snowflakes slicked off the cloaks Mrs Lappekonen had given them. Gerda lost all sense of direction, alone with Frida and Ba as the massive reindeer surged through a world of speed and noise and whirling weather.

6   The Snow Queen's Palace, a Mirror and its Pieces

Ba came to a halt, startling Gerda out of her thoughts. When had the snow stopped? Now Ba stood on a small hill in an icy landscape. Overhead the sky flamed and flickered with the weird shards and skeins of the Northern Lights.

On the next rise, the palace reared up before them, its impossibly high walls of snow glittering in the eerie light. They dismounted, and Ba roared a farewell as they marched forward. Then there was complete silence except for the packed snow squeaking and scrunching under their boots. Frida looked about them warily as they entered the palace. Gerda jumped as her friend drew her knife, but Frida was marking a trail by scratching on the ice walls.

They found their way inwards, still with nothing moving, nothing to stop them. At length they came to the Throne Room, and there was Kai, working silently at that puzzle.

'Kai!' shouted Gerda and dashed forward to him. She tried to hug him. He batted her away as if she was interfering with his game. But he was feeble. He was freezing cold.

'Kai, it's me, Gerda – I'm taking you home!' Gerda said brightly to him, trying to get his arm over her shoulders, to get him to his feet. 'We're going to ride on a reindeer, Kai – you'll be amazed – and get you to someone who can help ... '

Kai looked at her with complete indifference. He tried to go back to the puzzle.

'Oh, Kai, Kai!' Gerda wailed. The horror of seeing him like this, unable to care that they had come to save him, was suddenly just unbearable. She hugged him tight and sobbed into his chest.

Frida looked on helplessly. The hot sounds of human grief spilled out into that lifeless, uncaring place like a challenge. This sterile palace of hopelessness seemed to drink the noise up thirstily. To Frida it almost seemed that the walls were crowding in on them, listening, intent. She wiped her own tears, then ... 'Gerda!' she called.

Gerda looked up. She saw Kai's colour changing. He coughed. He groaned. He clawed at his chest. Something slipped through his fingers, and fell on the icy floor. The sound of the mirror shard landing was like a bell gone horribly wrong. Something about it pulled awfully at their hearing, a nasty, painful sound.

'Gerda ... Gerda?' said Kai. He clutched her to him. He didn't seem to be able to see. They were both weeping. 'Ah! My eye!' cried Kai, in pain. Again that icy horror of a noise, as another splinter came out. 'Gerda! It's you!' shouted Kai in his old voice now, the voice Gerda had not heard since that awful day at the carnival. 'You've come to save me! I always knew you would.'

They held each other for a while, weeping and laughing.

'The puzzle!' Kai said suddenly. 'Look!' And he carefully picked up one splinter, and fitted it into place. He cocked his head for a moment, looked at the puzzle, shifted the pieces, and then fitted in the second splinter. He gave Gerda a huge grin, but then it faded as he saw there was still a piece missing.

Frida stepped forward with a gentle smile. 'I expect this is why I'm here!' she said, opening the locket around her neck in which she carried her own mirror shard. As the locket opened, the mirror shard jumped into place in the puzzle – but the puzzle still had a long, lightning-shaped sliver missing.

'So now what … ?' began Frida, but she was stopped short. A huge howl, the roar of some enormous monster, echoed around the palace. The room shook. A small shower of ice crystals fell down from the roof.

'Run! It's the Snow Queen!' shouted Kai.

7 The Queen Unleashed:
A Puzzle and a Solution

They careered desperately through the passageways, Kai still clutching the puzzle, with the howl following them, echoing off the ice so that it was impossible to tell whether they were being chased or headed off.

Gasping for breath in the freezing air, the three of them stumbled out into the courtyard. But then they saw it, bounding towards them through the castle, claws scrabbling on the ice: a monster made of snow and ice, shaped like a huge arctic wolf, ridden by the Snow Queen. They dashed out of the gates towards Ba and safety.

But it was a hopeless race. They were barely half way to the ridge when the wolf overtook them ... was amongst them ... knocked Frida to the ground. Then it raised its massive head for a fatal bite.

Gerda hurled herself forwards. She grabbed the wolf's shoulder. There was a hiss, and her hands buried deep into the wolf, tearing apart the magic that bound the snow into wolf-form.

The wolf's whole leg sheared off and crumbled into snow. The stump gushed steaming melt-water. The wolf's roar turned into shrill yelps. It toppled away from Gerda and crashed to the ground, throwing up a cloud of snow and slush. When the snow settled, the Snow Queen lay at Gerda's feet.

Winded, gasping for breath, Frida got to her hands and knees in the snow. Knowing what could happen now with one mirror shard still at large – what must not happen – Frida crawled shakily towards the Snow Queen. The sound of Gerda's ragged breathing seemed unnaturally loud. *The Northern Lights are beginning to gather around Gerda,* Frida thought, *starting to pulse with her breathing*. Frida's world filled with that hypnotic, rasping and flashing – an intense power. A power she knew all too well from her robber days, trying to take her over again. She shook her head. Kai was crouched in the snow, grimacing, his eyes clenched shut, hands over his ears. The Snow Queen looked to be almost hypnotized, motionless at Gerda's feet. And Gerda? In the weird lighting Gerda was first silhouetted like a towering figure, then lit by the manic lights – her eyes flashing red or icy blue. She stared down at them – frighteningly inscrutable, raising her hands, slow as a glacier, fingers forming claws.

Frida reached for the Snow Queen. She pulled herself up, grabbed the locket from around her own neck and pulled it over the Snow Queen's unresisting head. Frida pushed the locket against the Snow Queen's chest. Nothing!

'Help me, Gerda!' Frida panted. 'It's not … working. Help her!'

Gerda stirred. The Northern Lights flashed and spun sickeningly. A half-smile appeared on Gerda's face. She stretched out one hand, palm open, towards the Snow Queen. Had Gerda heard, Frida wondered?

A jagged spark of scarlet light suddenly arced between Gerda's outstretched hand and the Snow Queen's chest. Both of them cried out in pain. The Snow Queen fell back. Gerda gasped, staggered, and clutched her hand. It was dripping blood, and was holding the Snow Queen's own mirror shard.

'No!' Frida gasped. She lunged over, half crawled, half climbed her way up Gerda's legs, grabbing Gerda's wrist, dragging that shard down, away from Gerda's heart.

'It's all right,' Gerda croaked. 'I'm not going to ... ' She blinked, shuddered – fighting the pain in her hand, or something in her head? Her eyes cleared. 'Where's the puzzle?' she asked urgently.

Kai had it. He held it out. The mirror shard on Gerda's hand began to shake, to slide towards the puzzle making a shrill chittering sound. Suddenly it flew across the gap and fixed itself into the puzzle. The chittering grew too shrill to bear, then suddenly stopped. Kai yelped and dropped the puzzle in the snow: it had burned his hand. The puzzle steamed and hissed venomously. Then it was done. The Hobgoblin's mirror had been reformed. Kai looked sidelong at it with revulsion, then threw his cloak over it. He wrapped it inside the cloak, knotting it firmly.

Gerda had sunk to her knees, clutching her wounded hand. Frida began to tear a strip off her cloak to bind it, but the Snow Queen reached out, and gently took Gerda's hand. Gerda started back as if stung, but her hand was healed – her palm now only had the faint, jagged, ice-blue scar she would keep all her life. She worked her fingers, wonderingly.

The Snow Queen was feeling the hem of the cloak Mrs Lappekonen had given Gerda.

'She sent you?' the Snow Queen asked. Gerda nodded.

'She will know how to end this story – she is good at human things,' the Snow Queen said. 'I am not. I have learned enough of your kind to want to say … "thank you" and "I'm sorry". But now I have my work to do in the world, and you have yours.' She raised her hands high and was suddenly the middle of a whirlwind of snow. The Northern Lights flowed down to meet the whirlwind, turning amber, gold … and then they, and it, and the Snow Queen were gone.

'"Not good at human things" … ?' echoed Kai.

'She's the spirit of the snow and ice and the white

wolves howling down the winter wind,' answered Gerda. 'Those are not human things. She has her own world. Without the mirror shard to make her cruel, she really has little interest in us at all.'

Ba roared and thundered down the hill behind them. They bundled themselves onto his back. He raised his great head, roared again, and then surged away. The snow flew up around his hooves and enveloped them. They held on as he hurtled through the blizzard. At last there was a flame ahead in the distance. It got closer. All of a sudden they had come to a stop in Mrs Lappekonen's paddock, and Mrs Lappekonen was standing there, in front of a bonfire.

'The puzzle?' asked Mrs Lappekonen. 'Put it on the fire!'

Jumping down, Kai unclasped his cloak and threw it, with the puzzle that was knotted up in it, onto the bonfire. Poisonous green flames stabbed up. The fire flared. Then with a noise like a shriek, a fireball flew up out of the bonfire, followed by a cloud of oily black smoke. Then it was all over, and the fire was burning cheerfully, with nothing left of the puzzle, and Mrs Lappekonen was smiling at them.

'So that is how the story of *A Mirror and its Pieces* really ends!' said Kai. 'We were part of the true ending, Gerda!'

8 A Girl and a Boy – Again

Gerda and Kai had come at last to the outskirts of their own town. It was a beautiful evening, of an early and gentle spring. From where they stood at the edge of a wood near the town, Gerda and Kai could see their homes. Frida had decided to stay with Mrs Lappekonen as her apprentice, though she had promised that she would come and visit them. They had just dismounted Ba and seen him go. It was the end of their adventure, but the normal, familiar town before them now seemed dreamlike and strange. However much they longed to be home, it was hard to step back into that world after all that had happened.

High in an ash tree, the crow watched them silently as they walked the last half mile home. They reached Gerda's house, paused for a moment, then knocked. The door opened, someone screamed in shock and wonder, and in a moment Gerda and Kai were in the midst of a stampede of delighted, amazed people wanting to hug them.

A babble of joyful noise carried out through the still-open door. Neighbours began to appear on the balconies and the street. The celebration was spreading.

The crow nodded to itself, and watched a moment more. Then it turned its back on the town and took off for home, its black wings merging with the gathering evening.